Haunted London

by Rupert Matthews

A Phantom Beheaded

Gentle Reader, forget creaking doors and eerie footsteps in old neglected manor houses for surely no ghosts can be more terrifying than those which appear in and around the Tower of London.

Can one imagine, for instance, the blood-freezing screams of an old lady protesting her innocence as, hurled to the ground by burly guards, her head is hacked off by the headsman? The screams are heard even today.

The lady was Margaret Pole, Countess of Salisbury, executed May 27th 1541 on Tower Green. It was here that, for centuries, the more important traitors and rebels after having been escorted through the 'Traitors Gate' were executed. Those of noble blood were afforded the privilege of a beheading which was supposed to be the quickest method of execution then known.

Alas, now and then the headsmen were not as efficient as one could reasonably expect. The butchery that took place when the aged Countess met her unjust fate was perhaps the most horrifying.

The Countess of Salisbury, Richard III's niece, was escorted through the Traitors

BELOW: Those condemned for treachery or dissent were taken into the Tower through the Traitors Gate.

FAR RIGHT: Tower Green where innumerable executions took place.

RIGHT: The execution site on Tower Green; here stood the block on which the condemned were told to lay their heads.

Gate to be imprisoned in the Tower until the day of her execution. The dignified elderly lady was entirely innocent of any crime except that of being born a Plantagenet and, therefore, too close in line to the throne for the then king, Henry VIII, to tolerate. Henry, a Tudor, was an implacable enemy of the Plantagenets. The hereditary feud between the two families had endured since the Wars of the Roses. When the Countess was taken to Tower Green for her execution she declared loudly that she was innocent and told the axeman 'Take my head as best you can'. She then refused to kneel and place her head on the block. The resulting bloodbath is that which is replayed so often and so brutally.

Other victims of execution in the Tower were gentle in life and in spectral form. The ghost of the tragic Lady Jane Grey, beheaded in 1554 because her father-in-law, John Dudley, Earl of Northumberland, claimed she should be queen, is rarely seen. Most recently she flitted quietly from the Salt Tower, and badly frightened young Welsh Guardsman Johns who was on duty. His officer dismissed the tale as too commonplace to bother with.

Equally calm was the response met by Scots Guardsman Howden in 1966. On guard at Traitors Gate one evening he distinctly heard the crunching boots of a patrol approaching from beyond Bloody Tower Arch. No patrol was due, so Howden raised his rifle and advanced. The noise came closer, passed by him and receded but no patrol was seen. Only a penetrating chill blast accompanied the sounds. Howden reported the incident to his sergeant but he was as unmoved as Johns' officer had been.

Taking a somewhat stricter line was the officer who, in 1864, found one guardsman

LEFT: *The execution of Lady Jane Grey as depicted by the Victorian artist George Cruikshank.*

most haunted place in the Tower, itself the most haunted location in London. In addition to the white lady of 1864, there is a grey lady, seen indoors and only by women but no one knows who she is. A man in 15th-century dress strolls around upstairs and it may be his footsteps which thump up the staircase.

slumped on the ground near the Queens House. The indignant officer charged the man with being drunk on duty and hauled him off to a court martial. The hapless soldier claimed he was not drunk but scared silly by a lady in white who not only ignored his challenge to halt but calmly walked through his bayonet and himself! No doubt the officers sitting in judgement found such a story hard to believe. Then a number of other soldiers tumbled forward to say that they too had seen the lady but had not wanted to report a ghost. Clearly the guard was popular with his mates.

The Queens House is very probably the

FAR LEFT: *Bloody Tower Arch where a phantom patrol was heard.*

LEFT: *A Guardsman on duty one night saw the spectral form of Lady Jane Grey leave the Salt Tower.*

Guy Fawkes was tortured in the Queens House after failing in his attempt to blow up Parliament in 1605. His screams are still heard occasionally. The Queens House also claims to be haunted by Anne Boleyn, queen to Henry VIII who was executed for treason and adultery after a show trial. However, Anne Boleyn is also said to haunt at least four other places, so she is either as energetic in death as she was in life, or the Tudor lady in Queens House is somebody else.

FAR RIGHT: *The arrest of Guy Fawkes, whose failure to blow up King James I and his Parliament is celebrated with firework displays every year on November 5th.*

RIGHT: *The lamp that Guy Fawkes took into the Houses of Parliament on the night of November 4th 1605.*

BELOW: *The Queens House is reported to be the most haunted place in the Tower of London.*

For visitors to the Tower of London there are plenty of other ghosts and phantoms for which to keep an eye and ear open. Sir Walter Raleigh walks the ramparts; screams come from the White Tower; an Elizabethan gentleman lurks in Bell Tower; a procession of knights marches in the Chapel of St Peter ad Vincula; the 8th Earl of Northumberland flits around Martin Tower and a giant

form of a huddled woman glowing faintly in the gutter. It is probably the sad ghost of Mary Ann Nicholls who became famous for being the first victim of Jack the Ripper in the long hot summer of 1888. She could have well done without such fame and Durward St could have done without its ghost which startled horses before the days of cars.

The identity of Jack the Ripper, who murdered five unfortunate women in the East End between April 1888 and July 1889, has never really been satisfactorily revealed. It is perhaps worth recording that when the landlord of a public house in Commercial Street learned that the body of the Ripper's second victim, Annie Chapman, had been discovered behind the pub he renamed it the 'Jack the Ripper'. Strangely, the maiden name of the landlord's wife was Chapman. A coincidence indeed! He often claimed that the 'Jack the Ripper' was haunted.

ABOVE: *The Church of All Hallows was once haunted by a white cat.*

BELOW: *Bucks Row (now Durward Street) is very different from the street which Jack the Ripper stalked.*

BELOW RIGHT: *The discovery of the body of Mary Ann Nichols on the night of August 31st 1888.*

bear stomps in the courtyard. The Tower is as full of ghosts as it is of tourists.

The phantoms come almost as thick and fast outside the Tower as within it. In a way, this is surprising for much of London was destroyed during the Blitz of 1940 and more has fallen to developers since. Yet this hardly seems to have bothered the

ghosts. The only famous spectre not to remain is the white cat which gambolled in the Church of All Hallows by the Tower in Great Tower Street. It has not been seen since the German Luftwaffe inconsiderately took away its home with an incendiary bomb on December 29th 1940.

At the heart of the East End is the more durable spectre of Durward St (once Bucks Row) in Whitechapel which seems to have survived the heavy bombing in World War II. The pathetic phantom takes the

A more genial ghost is to be found south of the Thames at Greenwich. In the 17th century, Greenwich echoed with scandalous tales of the great Lord Angosteen. Each night Lord Angosteen would dress in his finest lace and velvet before leaving to impress the ladies and indulge in heavy drinking and eating with his friends. Each morning, as dawn crept along the Thames, his coach would arrive to take him to his mansion on Shooters Hill. Many a milkman and early riser has been surprised by the spectral coach racing up Vanbrugh Hill with the merry lord in the back. It is good to know that there is in Greenwich a spirit that can be relied upon to have a good time.

Somewhat more substantial, is the old lady who frequents the Nag's Head on the Hackney Road to the north. She has the disconcerting habit of staring at people with penetrating eyes. Despite detailed descriptions of the lady, who wears Victorian dress, nobody has recognised her.

An elderly Victorian lady who can be identified is Sarah Whitehead. She haunts no less a building than the Bank of England. Indeed, some have suggested that the Bank's nickname, The Old Lady of Threadneedle Street, actually refers to the ghost. Poor Miss Whitehead was in the habit — in happier days — of waiting outside the Bank each evening for her brother who worked there. Then, in 1811, Mr Whitehead was convicted of fraud on such a scale as to lead to his execution. The shock was too much for his sister who became deranged. On many evenings she would turn up at the Bank dressed in

FAR LEFT: *A phantom coach is to be seen speeding up Vanbrugh Hill at dawn, with a revelling lord inside.*

BELOW: *Miss Sarah Whitehead, the original Old Lady of Threadneedle Street, who would often wait outside the Bank for her dead brother (from an old print).*

LEFT: *Bank of England.*

black, to meet her brother. Kindly Bank employees became used to escorting her home to her family. Then, in 1845, she died. Imagine the surprise of Bank employees when her spirit returned to the doors in the evenings to wait for her brother! She seems to have remained active for many years but has not been seen for some time. We can only hope she has now joined her beloved brother.

Rather more active in recent years is the ghostly clergyman of St Magnus the Martyr Church which stands in Fish Street Hill, (formerly New Fish Street) next to London Bridge. It conveniently potters around the tomb of Miles Coverdale and indeed fits his description. Born in 1488, Coverdale rose to be Bishop of Exeter before being removed by Catholic Mary I after he translated the Bible from Latin into English. When Protestant Elizabeth I came to the throne he was not reappointed bishop for political reasons, but the Queen made him rector of St Magnus both to give him a living and to keep him near the court. He died in 1569 and the hauntings began soon after.

Religious intolerance also lurks behind the hauntings of Smithfield. Out of London, Smithfield is best known as home to the finest meat market in Europe. It opens at midnight and closes early in the morning. The meat pitchers never seem to be disturbed by the ghostly moans which often echo around Smithfield where

religious offenders were burnt at the stake in Tudor times. Catholics and Protestants met gruesome deaths here.

Opposite Smithfield stands St Bartholomew the Great, the church which gave its name to the famous modern hospital. Both were founded as part of an Augustinian monastery by Prior Rahere, one time jester-minstrel at the court of King Henry I.

The Lady Chapel of St Bartholomew's is frequented by a very solid looking ghost

wearing a long cloak. Most often seen in the early morning, the phantom appears so real that more than one person has tried talking to it, thinking it to be a churchwarden. It is generally assumed the ghost is that of Rahere.

FAR LEFT: *The interior of St Magnus the Martyr.*

LEFT: *The tomb of Prior Rahere, one-time jester.*

BELOW: *The Church of St Bartholomew the Great.*

'Scratching Fanny'

RIGHT: *Amen Corner where, in the 18th century, the bodies of executed criminals were buried in unmarked graves.*

Cock Lane was once the talk of London Society. In the 18th century, a now vanished house was troubled by 'Scratching Fanny', a phantom who scratched and banged on walls and threw articles around the house. Fashionable ladies and gentlemen flocked to the house to watch the various manifestations, which stopped as suddenly as they had begun.

'Scratching Fanny' is now recognised as a classic poltergeist. These spirits are said to manifest themselves around a teenager, usually a girl, and can cause havoc in a household.

Though Cock Lane is now bereft of ghosts, St Paul's Cathedral is not. The quiet spirit there is that of a religious man, though he is never seen clearly enough to reveal whether he is a warden or a priest. His favourite spot seems to be in the Kitchener Chapel, though he may flit around the entire western end of the cathedral.

Barely a stone's throw away is Greyfriar's Churchyard where ghost-hunters have a choice of several phantoms. But only a truly brave person would seek out the repulsive 'thing' in Amen Corner. The curiously named Amen Corner lies off Ave Maria Lane by Ludgate Hill. The hideous black shape which squirms around this place at night exudes an atmosphere of intense evil and threat, so can have little to do with the pious names of the locale. A more likely connection is the fact that this was the spot beside Newgate Prison where criminals executed at Tyburn in the 18th century were buried in unmarked graves. It would not be wise to pass this way at night. Fortunately Amen Corner is a cul-de-sac so the unwary passerby is unlikely to wander inadvertently into the lair of the 'thing'.

To outsiders the Temple, off Fleet Street, to the west of the City, is a strange private place. The buildings are virtually unaltered by over two centuries of use. Most bewildering of all is the mass of wigs and gowns which flit by as the lawyers go about their business.

In such a place a stranger would be forgiven if he failed to notice that one gowned and bewigged figure was any different from the rest. Insiders though, can spot Baron Brampton at a glance. His collar and cravat are of an ancient cut and his feet make no noise on the flagstones!

Born humble Henry Hawkins, Brampton earned his barony by his skill as a lawyer which amounted to near genius. He was called to the bar in 1843, at the age of 26, and spent almost the rest of his life in and around the Temple. His moment of glory was in 1873 with the Tichbourne Case.

BELOW: *Old St Paul's before the Great Fire of London (from an old print).*

LEFT: *The Temple is haunted by the ghost of a 19th-century judge.*

to stalk the corner of old London which saw his greatest triumphs.

A short distance to the north, in the Royal Free Hospital in Grays Inn Road, another professional returns to her place of work but for more gruesome reasons. The corridors and back stairs used by staff are haunted by a Victorian nurse who hanged herself in the clothes store. No reason for this tragic suicide is known.

Between the hospital and the river lies Red Lion Square. The three distinguished ghosts who haunt the Square were close in life, and closer still in death, but their ghosts are rarely seen together. These are Oliver Cromwell, Henry Ireton and John Bradshaw.

This great affair centred around an Australian butcher named Arthur Orton who claimed to be Roger Tichbourne, and so heir to a vast fortune and a title. Hawkins appeared for the prosecution when Orton was charged with perjury and fraud, and he was brilliant. So complex was the evidence that the trial dragged on for 188 days in court over a period of three years. It was after this marathon that Hawkins became a judge and in 1899 a baron. It is little wonder that Baron Brampton returns

LEFT: *Henry Ireton, Oliver Cromwell's soldier son-in-law.*

ABOVE: *The spiked head of Oliver Cromwell (from a contemporary print).*

RIGHT: *The ghost of a grey nurse has been seen recently in St Thomas's Hospital.*

RIGHT: *A frightening doppelganger once stalked the corridors of the Palace of Westminster.*

Oliver Cromwell, of course, was in general largely responsible for the victory of Parliament in the Civil War. In January 1649 he ordered the execution of the king, Charles I, allegedly for treason but in reality to tighten Cromwell's own hold on power. From then until his death in 1658, Cromwell ruled England with an iron fist. Ireton was a brilliant general in his own right. He served as Cromwell's second-in-command and his deputy in Ireland. John Bradshaw, meanwhile, was a lawyer with a ferocious attachment to Parliament. Cromwell chose Bradshaw to be president of the court which tried King Charles and it was John Bradshaw who delivered the sentence of death. He died one year after Cromwell.

When Charles II returned to claim his father's throne in 1660, he pardoned many who fought for Parliament, but not Cromwell, Ireton and Bradshaw. Their bodies were exhumed and hanged at Tyburn, as befitted traitors, before being thrown into a common grave beside the gibbet. Cromwell's head was spiked on Westminster Hall for good measure. Their reason for haunting Red Lion Square has never been discovered.

Stretching for two miles from the Thames at Westminster Palace to Kensington Palace is a straggling line of royal, public and private premises which host a gallery of strange, horrific and quirky phantoms. This is London's 'ghostly crescent'.
The most southerly of this parade of ghosts is found in St Thomas's Hospital on the South Bank. The grey nurse began her hauntings in late Victorian times, but nobody was ever certain who she was. Some claimed she was a nurse who died of a disease caught from a patient, others that she was a nurse who committed suicide after being severely reprimanded by a particularly vicious sister and some even claimed she was Florence Nightingale. The grey nurse was invariably accompanied by a chill, damp atmosphere and sometimes a feeling of worry or concern.

Much of St Thomas's Hospital has been redeveloped, but the ghost was clearly seen in June 1992 by a sister on a late duty. Returning to her ward after dealing with

some paperwork, the sister saw a lady in a long grey dress in the corridor ahead of her. Thinking the figure to be a real person who had somehow lost her way, the sister called out. The figure ignored her and instead peered into a ward. The sister approached and was about to ask the woman her business, when the strange

figure melted away into nothingness. Only then did the sister realise that she had seen the ghost frequently talked about during the four years she had so far spent at St Thomas's.

From St Thomas's it is possible to gaze across the Thames to the Palace of Westminster, scene of a most curious haunting. For some years in the 1920s a Mr Milman was one of the many staff who lived in the Palace. His wife lived there, too, and so began the trouble. Mrs Milman had a fetch or doppelganger, a spectral copy of herself which had a life and will of its own. The existence of the fetch first came to light when a House Steward saw Mrs Milman strolling on the ground floor and, only moments later, found her upstairs resting.

Thereafter, the very solid-looking fetch was glimpsed many times by the staff. It was identical to the real Mrs Milman in all ways but two. The fetch never spoke, and ignored people who spoke to it, as if deaf.

Secondly, it seemed to delight in doing the opposite to whatever the real Mrs Milman was attempting. For instance, when Mrs Milman was locking doors for the night in one part of the Palace, the fetch was happily throwing them open elsewhere. After some months of intense activity, the fetch was seen less frequently and eventually walked no more, much to the relief of the hapless Mrs Milman.

Just over the road from Westminster Palace is Westminster Abbey. Founded by King Edward the Confessor in the 11th century and rebuilt in stages from 1250 to 1740, this ancient building contains the bones of many famous people, but it has only three ghosts.

ABOVE: *There are said to be three ghosts in Westminster Abbey.*

LEFT: *Does a sinister monk haunt the Little Cloister of Westminster Abbey?*

A Mysterious Monk

ABOVE: *In Westminster Cathedral a tall sombre figure was seen lurking near the high altar.*

Perhaps the only act of violence in the Abbey is commemorated by a ghost. A phantom monk flits around the quiet cloisters, usually in the early evening during autumn as the weak sun leaves the gardens. He is said to be rather tall and many witnesses report the contempt in the spirit's eyes. For centuries nobody knew who he was, but assumed correctly that he dated from the period when the Abbey really was an abbey. Then, in 1934, the aged ghost spilled the beans to a psychic investigator who was, apparently, the first person ever to speak to him. The monk said his name was Benedictus and that he had been murdered while trying to stop a gang of city toughs from robbing the Abbey. The religious difficulties of Henry VIII's reign had, seemingly, led the Protestant youths to lose respect for the Church and so plan the robbery. Unfortunately for this neat story, the Abbey records are intact and show neither robbery nor murder.

The nave of the Abbey has, in more recent years, been home to a ghostly soldier.

Clad in khaki and of World War I vintage, he is said to be sad and approaches people as if about to ask a question before vanishing. Inevitably perhaps, he has been dubbed the Unknown Warrior. The third ghost, and the least often seen, is that of Oliver Cromwell's associate John Bradshaw, who also haunts Red Lion Square. Bradshaw lurks in the deanery more often than in the Abbey proper.

Westminster Cathedral, the 1910 Catholic church, was the scene of a ghost sighting in the 1960s. A tall, black-clad figure was seen moving around the high altar. The ghost, if that is what it was, has never been seen since, and it was very late on a dark night. Also glimpsed only once and at dead of night was the headless woman of Scotland Yard. She flitted into the Black Museum in Parliament Street late one night and badly startled the night watchman. The Black Museum houses a collection of murder weapons and other evidence kept by the force, so perhaps she was connected with one of the gruesome objects.

More persistent is the phantom of Vine Street Police Station, just off Piccadilly Circus. Sergeant Goddard hanged himself in a cell during the reign of King Edward VII for some unknown reason and has returned many times. He is seen from time to time but has become the target for blame if ever anything goes wrong. Muddled papers, lights left on and unlocked doors have all been attributed to Sergeant Goddard. One cannot help wondering if the poor sergeant has become rather a useful ghost for overtired policemen.

A short walk west of Vine Street is what was once the most notorious and horrific haunted house in London, 50 Berkeley Square. It long had the reputation of being an evil house and many tales were told to substantiate this. The fact that, for so many years, the house stood empty probably had much to do with the stories.

LEFT: *A police sergeant who committed suicide haunts Vine Street police station.*

BELOW LEFT: *Berkeley Square, where grand facades may conceal horrible secrets.*

Tales of unnatural happenings began when William IV was on the throne, but the hauntings intensified in the 1860s. The house had recently been left by an elderly lady to an eccentric man who discouraged visitors. Some said the nameless horror began when a young woman killed herself rather than accept the advances of a lecherous guardian, others that a lunatic heir had been incarcerated in the house by a younger brother who took his inheritance. Whatever the origins of the terror, it was enough to send two sailors running from the house at midnight after they had broken into the empty building for somewhere to sleep. Lord Lyttleton stayed one night and saw a 'thing' at which he shot. More than one Victorian lady visiting the premises fainted after being overcome by an unreasoning fear. The phantom, whatever it was, seems to have left. The building is now an office and the staff experience no nameless fears, except perhaps too much overtime.

ABOVE: *50 Berkeley Square was reputedly the most haunted house in London.*

South of Berkeley Square lies St James's Palace, to which ambassadors are still accredited although the Royal Family lives at Buckingham Palace. This ancient building is frequented by a particularly gruesome phantom. A man, in the court dress of the early 19th century, patters around the private apartments with his head lolling precariously to one side exposing an ugly slit across his throat. The spectre is presumed to be that of Sellis, valet to Ernest Augustus, Duke of Cumberland and fifth son of George III.

Sellis cut his own throat late one night in 1810 after he launched a frenzied attack on his royal master. The reasons for this violent behaviour are unknown, though gossip-mongers at the time suggested that Cumberland had seduced Sellis's pretty teenage daughter.

The Duke's other valet, summoned to the scene, stated that Cumberland was standing with his shirt blood-stained and a sword with a bloody blade lying on the floor. Rumours spread to the effect that the Duke had murdered his valet to shut his mouth about the Duke's seduction of his daughter. Cumberland had never been popular with the London crowd so such tales were bound to emerge. Soon after, Cumberland travelled to the Continent to fight in the wars against Napoleon. In 1837, he became King of Hanover. Sellis, however, remained at home to stalk the corridors of St James's Palace.

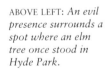

ABOVE LEFT: *An evil presence surrounds a spot where an elm tree once stood in Hyde Park.*

LEFT: *The spectre of a man with a slashed throat patters around in St James's Palace.*

At the far end of The Mall stands Buckingham Palace, the present residence of the monarch. The Palace is very much a private home and not a place about which 'supernatural' gossip arises in profusion but one ghost tale will not go away. The building of the huge house was started by John Sheffield, Duke of Buckingham and Normanby, who managed the neat trick of being on good terms with both the autocratic James II and the man who overthrew him, William III. The ghost, though, goes back long before the house was built, for the site was occupied by a priory in medieval times and it is a monk who flits around the gardens. Few people report seeing the phantom these days, but that may be due to tact and good manners where royalty is concerned rather than to any lack of sightings.

A few steps to the south stand the Wellington Barracks in Birdcage Walk. It was here, in the 1780s, that a guardsman murdered his wife and disposed of her body in St James's Park. Her ghostly figure still makes the journey from the barracks to the park, usually when there is not much traffic around, which is not very often these days.

The other great royal park, Hyde Park, also has its ghosts. The phantom horse-bus which trundles along the northern boundary is sometimes not recognised for what it is. So solid does the bus appear that some have mistaken it for a tourist attraction. More dangerous is the evil presence which lurks around a spot where

an elm tree used to stand in the park. London tramps sleep in the parks but never near the spot. One woman tramp who did take a nap here in the 1930s died in her sleep. Several people have felt uneasy near the spot. Dutch elm disease has taken the tree but the unease remains.

At the opposite end of London's social scale was the phantom which graced a home in Hyde Park Place in 1884. The Leigh-Hunts were up in London for the social season that year and had rented the grand house in the hope of making an impression and perhaps attracting suitable husbands for their daughters. It was, however, the house which made the impression. Miss Kathleen was the first to speak of the ghostly maid whom she followed upstairs and then saw vanish. Soon other members of the family and their staff glimpsed the stranger. The phantom appeared perfectly solid and as if going about her usual housemaidly duties but she always vanished when approached. Before long the 'troubles' of the Leigh-Hunts became the society gossip and greatly enlivened the season. No husbands, though, were found for the daughters.

ABOVE LEFT: *A Guardsman murdered his wife in Wellington Barracks and her ghost now strolls nearby.*

ABOVE: *As soon as somebody noticed the phantom housemaid in the Leigh-Hunt home in Hyde Park Place she would vanish.*

A Sad Pale Face

ABOVE: *The ghost of King George II still waits at a window of Kensington Palace.*

At the western end of Hyde Park stands Kensington Palace. It is here that one of the most often seen and best authenticated Royal ghosts is to be found. George II lived his first 30 years in Hanover, the land of his ancestors, and came to Britain in 1714, 13 years before he became king. He remained firmly attached to his charming German state with its provincial relaxations and lack of worries.

As he lay dying in Kensington Palace in October 1760, he was expecting important news from Hanover. A brisk westerly wind kept the ships carrying his couriers in port and no message came. The king would frequently peer out of his window at the weathervane, hoping for the wind to change and muttering to himself. He died before the news that he craved arrived.

To this day his sad, pale face can be seen gazing up at the weathervane and asking the eternal question 'Why don't they come?'

Now let us return to the West End for a batch of highly active theatrical ghosts.

Actors are generally more associated with their places of work than with their homes and none more so than the popular Joseph Grimaldi. Born in 1779 to Italian parents living in London, Grimaldi took to the boards of the Sadler's Wells Theatre when still a boy. It was in this theatre that he achieved his greatest successes as a clown, specialising in a style of comic

dancing and facial movements which set the pattern for others. He had extremely powerful legs and was nicknamed 'Iron Legs'. In 1837 he died and almost immediately returned to haunt Sadler's Wells. His characteristic face was glimpsed in one of the boxes during performances. This, rather understandably, startled the performers who knew and recognised him. Grimaldi's ghost still has the power to shock today.

RIGHT: *Soon after he died, the ghost of the famous clown Joseph Grimaldi was seen in Sadlers Wells theatre.*

Also returning to a theatre after death, is the army officer who lurks in the dress circle of the Coliseum Theatre. Nobody seems quite certain who he is, but he began his hauntings in the last months of World War I and is dressed in the khaki uniform of the period. It is believed that this spirit is of an officer who enjoyed seeing shows here during his all too infrequent leaves from the Front and that he was killed during the war.

Sadly the St James's Theatre exists no longer. Built in 1835 it was demolished in 1957. In 1923 a seance was held in the theatre following an earlier seance, and for a very good reason. Both had been called by the Society for Psychical Research. An actress and two actors had attended the first seance when a phantom hand holding a pen suddenly appeared to them.

When asked by the medium to whom did the hand belong, it wrote: 'I am Oscar Wilde. I have come back to let the world know I am not dead. Death is the most boring thing in life, except marriage or dining with a schoolmaster.' A typical piece of Oscar Wilde drollery.

Understandably a second seance was arranged and on this occasion some of Wilde's elderly friends were asked to attend.

Again the ghostly hand appeared and after it had penned the answers to a few of the questions asked by Wilde's friends, it wrote a much longer message. It was full of the flowery romanticism to which Oscar had been so partial during his life on earth.

Such phrases as 'red sunset must follow the apple-green dawn' and 'year after year the hawthorn bears blood-red fruit after the white death of May' were strewn through the message which ended with the forlorn appeal 'Pity Oscar Wilde'.

Persecuted in his lifetime for his homosexual propensities, shunned by his former friends, dying in exile, many people these days do 'Pity Oscar Wilde'. Even on his death bed his wit did not desert him: 'Either that wallpaper goes or I do.'

LEFT: *The Coliseum Theatre, said to be haunted by a spectral officer from World War I.*

BELOW LEFT: *A phantom hand appeared at a seance in the St James's Theatre in 1923. Was it Oscar Wilde?*

BELOW: *A portrait of Oscar Wilde by Toulouse Lautrec.*

The ghost of the Adelphi Theatre is a chilling spectre. The hauntings started during the Edwardian era and took the form of a tall man with noticeably white gloves. The phantom was remarkably shy and nobody got close enough to identify him. That was solved in 1950 when a member of staff turned a corner in a corridor and came face to face with the ghost. The features of the spectre were clear and etched themselves on her memory. A short session with pictures of former actors and staff quickly solved the mystery. The ghost was William Terriss, heart-throb of the Victorian stage.

The reason for the haunting at once came to hand. Terriss had been savagely murdered by a lunatic outside the stage door while appearing with Jessie Milward in a successful long run at the Adelphi. The play was Secret Service. Terriss was playing the leading role and a supporting part was acted by an unbalanced man named Richard Arthur Prince who was jealous of and detested Terriss. Charged with murder the verdict was insanity and Prince died 40 years later in Broadmoor Prison.

The phantom Terriss has also been seen flitting around the Covent Garden Underground, which he used every evening to reach the theatre, retracing his steps to death.

Equally tragic is the spectre of the Theatre Royal, Drury Lane. The 'man in grey' only appears during daylight hours, startling

cleaners and matinee audiences alike. His dress is distinctive. He is attired as an 18th-century dandy with grey jacket, high riding boots and a snow white shirt rich with lace. The confident bearing and long stride mark him out as a man of distinction. In 1870 extensive rebuilding of the theatre revealed a blocked up recess which was torn open by the curious workmen. Inside was a crumpled skeleton with a dagger

ABOVE LEFT: *The Adelphi Theatre where the ghost of William Terriss has been seen.*

jammed between the ribs. The skeleton had fragments of clothing around it. The cloth was grey. Legend asserts that the phantom appears only during a long run.

The spectre of the great comedian Dan Leno has been glimpsed in the Theatre Royal. Leno first gained fame as the champion clog dancer of northern England, but then took to comedy. He appeared in the Theatre Royal pantomime every year from 1888 until his death in 1904.

One of the oldest of the theatrical ghosts with which London abounds is that of the great Regency beauty Sarah Siddons. Famous as an actress of great power and presence, Siddons lived at 228 Baker Street, where a London Transport electrical sub-station now stands.

The Haymarket Theatre has a ghost which, like the Theatre Royal's man in grey, is said to herald a successful show. The identity of this ghost, however, is well known. He is John Buckstone, the larger-than-life actor manager of the Haymarket from 1853 to 1876. Buckstone had the popular touch and put on a succession of melodramatic plays and uproarious farces which kept his theatre packed with the London crowd for as long as he lived. Perhaps it is that knack for picking a winner which enables him to return when a popular show is being staged.

Perhaps we should end this book on Britain's haunted capital with a remark of Oscar Wilde's. When told that he would have to pay a large sum for a serious operation, his reply was 'Ah, well then. I suppose I shall have to die beyond my means.'

ABOVE: *The ghost of the celebrated actress Sarah Siddons haunts the site of her former house.*

ABOVE: *The great actor, William Terriss with Jessie Milward, who was beside him when he died.*

BELOW: *A panorama of London characters.*

London in the sixteenth century

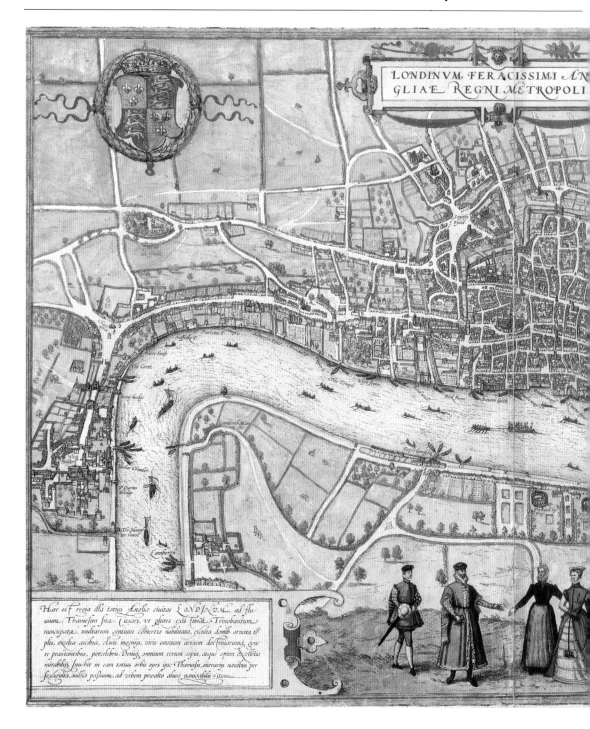

Westminster Abbey, Smithfield, the Tower and many other historic sites are clearly visible in this magnificent map.